Claire Austin
photography by Clay Perry

Iris
the classic bearded varieties

Viking Studio

VIKING STUDIO
Published by the Penguin Group
Penguin Putnam Inc., 375 Hudson Street,
New York, New York 10014,
U.S.A.

Penguin Books Ltd, Registered Offices:
Harmondsworth, Middlesex,
England

First published in the United States by Viking Studio,
a member of Penguin Putnam Inc.

First Printing, January 2002

10 9 8 7 6 5 4 3 2 1

Copyright © Text 2001 Claire Austin
Copyright © Special Photography 2001 Clay Perry
Copyright © Design and layout 2001 Quadrille Publishing Ltd

ISBN: 0-670-03034-1

Printed and bound in Singapore

contents

A passion for irises 4

Tall Bearded irises 10

Median irises 56

Bearded irises in the garden 84

Iris suppliers 102
Index 103
Acknowledgments 104

a passion for irises

The bearded iris is one of the world's most glamorous flowers and a popular garden plant. It is tough, easy to grow, and dramatic. In those who love it, it creates a lasting passion. In those less familiar with this beautiful flower, it inspires awe. The complex blooms are produced in an extraordinary array of colors and an endless variety of patterns and forms. Each large flower is carried on a sturdy, upright stem that erupts from a leafy clump of long, sword-shaped leaves. In a garden border, bearded irises are excellent for providing both color and architectural structure. Grow them and you will never be disappointed.

My first encounter with bearded irises was fifteen years ago. At that time I was working at the family nursery in Shropshire. Although primarily a rose grower and breeder, my father had also gathered together a large number of herbaceous garden plants. Many of these had large and dramatic flowers, and they included bearded irises. Since I was trained as a book illustrator, it was these that caught my imagination.

The initial iris collection contained plants from many sources. Some were rescued from Kew Gardens in London when their once-famous iris borders were being dismantled; other hybrids were collected from nurseries around Britain and the United States. A number were bought directly from their breeders. However, since that time the collection has evolved and many new varieties have been added. Older hybrids, no longer relevant to the gardener or even to the iris historian, have been discarded. The collection now contains more than four hundred varieties, most of which are sold through our mail-order catalog.

Choosing from so many varieties can be incredibly difficult, even for an iris enthusiast. There are literally thousands of hybrids available around the world today. Not even the most dedicated grower can be familiar with every one, and another iris enthusiast might have chosen to include a different selection from mine. This book is designed not only to help the gardener choose which bearded irises to grow, but also to show how diverse in form and color their flowers can be. In putting together my selection, I hope to demonstrate how these beautiful plants have developed over the last hundred years.

Each variety included in the book has been selected for specific reasons. Firstly, it may be of historical importance in the development of the iris. Then it might be a handsome representative of its type, be that tall or small. All the varieties included must, however, also be good garden plants. Finally, they should be easy to purchase. Ultimately, of course, this selection can only be a snapshot of what is available today. However, I have grown every variety included here and know them all to be excellent plants.

A family of irises

The bearded iris is just one member of the large and diverse genus *Iris*, in the family Iridaceae. The genus contains over three hundred named species; some of these are bulbous, others rhizomatous. All originated in the Northern Hemisphere, but their natural environments differ greatly from one another. Some require conditions as arid as those of northern Africa, while others grow in wet areas such as bogs and along the edges of streams. There are types that will grow in shade and others that will tolerate nothing less than full sun.

The bearded iris

The bearded iris gets its name from the "beard" found toward the back of the lower petals. Made up of short hairs, it looks very much like a long, furry caterpillar; its purpose is to guide pollinating insects toward the reproductive parts of the plant.

The wild forms of bearded iris can be found growing in a large region that stretches from central Europe down to the Arabian Peninsula, and from Spain across to Asia. Only the hardiest of these have been used to produce our garden hybrids. These wild forms are species that naturally grow in open areas with hot summers and very cold winters, making them incredibly tough garden plants. All require a soil that is well drained and receives full sun for most of the day. And all the irises in this book can be grown in US zones 3 to 8.

The flower

Bearded irises are grown mainly for their beautiful, if somewhat delicate flowers. All irises produce blooms with six large petals. Of these, three—the standards—grow upright. These give the tall varieties one of their common names, the flag iris. The three lower petals are called falls, which describes them perfectly.

The flowers come in a variety of shapes and sizes. Many have petals that are laced or ruffled around the edges, others are smooth and delicate. Some are no more than 2 inches (5cm) across, while others grow as large as 8 inches (20cm).

Color

The flowers of bearded irises come in a rainbow of colors. These range from pure white and creamy yellow to bright yellow and vivid orange. There are red-browns and chestnut-browns, but sadly no true reds. There are blues that are nearly white through to almost black, with the "black" varieties varying from very dark blue to dark purple.

Colors are also blended and mixed into many further variations. Some varieties have petals of two different hues; some have color stippled and splashed over the petals; others feature layers of color blended one over another. To help define these variations, the color types have been divided into named groups. The list that follows explains those that are most commonly used.

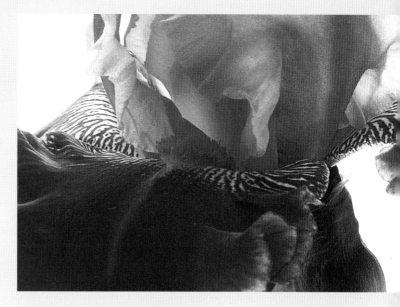

Amoena
White standards and darker-colored falls, usually blue or purple.

Bicolor
Standards and falls in two different colors.

Bitone
Standards and falls in the same color, but in two different shades.

Blend
Flowers in a multitude of colors, usually too sophisticated or unusual to place elsewhere.

Neglecta
Pale blue standards with dark blue or violet falls.

Plicata
Complicated, subtle, and often exotic, with a background of either yellow or white over which a second color is stitched or stippled.

Self
Flowers in one color only.

Height

The bearded iris not only varies in flower color, but also in plant size: they can grow from only 6 inches (15cm) high right up to 4 feet (120cm). For easy recognition of these different height types, they have been broken down into six groups that are accepted internationally.

Median

This section includes varieties that grow from 6 inches (15cm) up to 28 inches (70cm) high. They make excellent border plants and flower from mid-spring to early summer. This section is further divided into five distinct groups.

Miniature Dwarf Bearded (MDB) Height: 6–8 inches (15–20cm)
Flower size: 1½–3¼ inches (4–8cm) across
Flowering period: Early spring

Standard Dwarf Bearded (SDB) Height: 8–16 inches (20–40cm)
Flower size: 2–3 inches (5–7cm) across
Flowering period: Late spring

Intermediate Bearded (IB) Height: 16¼–28 inches (41–70cm)
Flower size: 4–5¼ inches (10–13cm) across
Flowering period: Late spring to early summer

Border Bearded (BB) Height: 16¼–28 inches (41–70cm)
Flower size: 4–5¼ inches (10–13cm) across
Flowering period: Late spring to early summer

Miniature Tall Bearded (MTB) (also known as Table Irises)
Height: 16¼–28 inches (41–70cm)
Flower size: 2–3¼ inches (5–8cm) across
Flowering period: Late spring to early summer

Tall (TB)

This is the most majestic group as well as the most popular. They are the tallest and latest flowering of all bearded irises.

Height: 28 inches to 4 feet (70–120cm)
Flower size: 4–8 inches (10–20cm)
Flowering period: Early summer, divided into early, mid-, and late season

Flower of the world

There are a great many accounts of how the iris came by its name. All agree that its origins lie in Greek mythology and that it is named after the Rainbow Goddess, Iride or Iris. All the tales are wonderfully romantic, but they differ slightly in detail. The most commonly told explains how Iris, the messenger of the gods, scattered fields full of irises with the colors of the rainbow as she passed messages between heaven and earth.

The iris has a long and varied history. As early as the fifteenth century it was grown commercially for its rhizomes. When dried, these produce orris, a substance used in the production of powders and perfumes. The irises most commonly grown for this purpose were the wild types, *I. florentina* (known as orris root), *I. germanica*, and *I. pallida*, often called the blue flag iris. In some areas of Europe it was a very important crop. The city of Florence, for example, depicted the iris on its coins, and even today a red iris appears on Florence's coat of arms. In medieval times the iris also found its way into the royal coat of arms of France and England, in the form of the fleur-de-lis—a stylized iris.

Neither was the beauty of the iris overlooked. The ancient Minoans painted irises on murals around the walls of their great buildings. In Luxor, the ancient Egyptian temples featured paintings of irises, while the marble walls around the Taj Mahal in India have elegantly carved iris flowers.

However, the types depicted in these works were almost always beardless irises. The bearded iris came to be celebrated much later in sixteenth- and seventeenth-century Dutch masterpieces, although perhaps their most famous representation is in paintings by Monet. Monet was an enthusiastic grower of irises and used his garden at Giverny in France as the subject for many of his paintings. Other artists have followed suit, and perhaps the most famous of these is the modern Scottish artist Elizabeth Blackadder. Her delicate interpretation of the bearded iris is a strong feature of many of her watercolor paintings.

Developing the flower

Over the past century the development of the bearded iris has been tremendous. At the beginning of this period the flowers came in only white, yellow, or purple, or occasionally a combination of all three colors. This often resulted in a murky blend of muted shades. Since then, hybridizers have expanded the range into a vast rainbow of colors—and as the number of tones has increased, so has the size of the flower. Because of this, the petals, which once were smooth and delicate in shape, are now of necessity ruffled, fluted, and thick in substance.

Modern developments

The earliest bearded iris hybrids date back to the early 1800's and were raised in Britain and France from seedlings selected by nurserymen from naturally occurring open-pollinated crosses. It soon became apparent that an incredible number of variations could occur, so by the beginning of the twentieth century, nurseries were embarking seriously on full-blown breeding programmes. As a consequence, the bearded iris rapidly developed beyond all recognition and by the middle of the twentieth century hundreds of new plants were being introduced each year. Most of these were of dubious merit and tended to disappear quickly. Those that survived did so because they were both robust and beautiful, and many remain popular with gardeners and nurserymen today.

Above This beautiful variety—*Iris* 'Skier's Delight'—demonstrates what breeders of the modern Tall Bearded iris are aiming for. Both the falls and standards are even in size and ruffled around the edges. This ruffling is not just decorative: it also strengthens the petals against severe weather conditions.

Irises are bred in many countries, but today the majority come from nurseries in the United States. The immense influence of American hybridizers began to be felt during World War II, when most Europeans were not able to afford the cost or time involved in plant hybridization. With no competition, American iris breeders began to develop the bearded iris into the plant it is today—large and defiantly flamboyant.

After the war, hybridizers in other countries returned to breeding plants. The iris has now become a global flower, with breeders working in many parts of the world, including the UK, France, Australia, Italy, and Germany. Despite this, American varieties are still extremely influential, and almost all today's new hybrids contain some "blood" from American varieties.

Societies, shows and awards

There are many iris societies and groups worldwide, and they all hold at least one iris show a year. The current list extends to the United States, Canada, the UK, Australia, New Zealand, France, Belgium, Denmark, Switzerland, Italy, Japan, South Africa, and Russia. The first to be established was the American Iris Society in 1920.

The societies' aim is to exchange information, air opinions, and give awards to outstanding plants. At one time, competition for awards led to the introduction of varieties with large flowers on strong, upright stems that looked excellent in a vase, but were poor performers in the garden. The flowers were often damaged in bad weather, and the growing energy of the plant was directed into the production of flowers rather than foliage, so the plants were left weak and susceptible to disease. However, over the last twenty years, iris breeders have gotten back on track, and the more recent introductions are proving to be as good in the garden as on the show stands.

Recently introduced varieties are judged for the quality of the foliage and flower after having been grown in trial grounds for several seasons. Some are general horticultural awards given by a horticultural society: in the United States, the American Horticultural Society gives the award of Horticultural Merit (HM); in the UK, the Royal Horticultural Society gives the Award of Garden Merit (AGM). Other awards are more specific to irises. In Italy, the highest award that can be given to an iris is the Premio Firenze. The top award given in America, the UK, and Australia is the Dykes Medal (DM)—named after W. R.

Dykes, the first plantsman to categorize the whole genus. The Dykes Medal is given on behalf of the British Iris Society, but judging is by the iris societies of the individual countries.

Choosing and buying

Medals may help the average iris buyer to select a variety, but these are awarded to a very limited number of plants each year. With so many to choose from, it is difficult to know where to begin. The first step is to find a nursery that stocks a good range of bearded irises. Any growers worth their salt will list only plants they know are good—a good variety is one that is worthy of a place in the garden and must therefore be reliable, robust, and attractive in both flower and foliage.

Plants are better purchased bare rooted—dug straight from the ground—from iris specialists, rather than in containers from gardening centers. They will then be planted at the right time— from summer, after they have flowered, up until early fall, which will get them off to a better start in life. Many nurseries now have websites to complement their mail-order catalogs, and as a result plant-buying has become international. Each year I import many new varieties into the UK from both France and the United States. This is an exciting and, these days, relatively easy process. However, many of these will never have been grown outside their country of origin, and for the general gardener it may be more sensible—and less expensive—to purchase plants from a nursery based in their own country.

Above *Iris* 'Alizes', a handsome French variety, was introduced in 1989, but it was not until 2000 that it was awarded an AGM by the British Iris Society after being grown in trials in the Royal Horticultural Society gardens in Surrey, England.

Above The Standard Dwarf bearded irises are very different in shape from their taller sisters. The petals are smaller and the standards arch over. This *Iris* 'Truly' is a perfect example of its group.

tall
bearded irises

Tall Bearded irises, occasionally referred to as flag or German irises, comprise the tallest group of bearded irises. This category contains the largest number of hybrids, in the widest variety of colors. Many are flamboyant, in bright hues; others are tranquil, in gentle pastel shades. The blooms unfurl from long buds, one at a time, to form an elegant, upright stem of flowers. At any one time this spike might carry up to six blooms, and as each fades, more emerge. At the base is a slowly spreading, spiky clump of long, sword-shaped leaves. The foliage is reason enough to include the bearded iris in the garden border, as it makes an excellent contrast to plants with fluffy, deeply divided, or rounded foliage. Planted in small groups, Tall Bearded irises add a splash of color among leafy shrubs and perennials. In drifts, they provide a statuesque swathe of color that draws the eye into the landscape. However you decide to plant them, these beautiful irises are easy to grow and suitable for all styles and sizes of garden.

Latin Rock

The colors of many modern bearded irises are not found in older hybrids. These were only produced in primary and secondary colors; some were a muddy blend of both and looked as if the artist had failed to wash the paintbrush between the applications of different colors. As a result, they blended well with other flowers and never dominated the garden. Modern varieties such as this one can be extremely "individual" and difficult to incorporate among other plants. In color, Latin Rock is exotic. Its standards are peach-pink washed with soft purple, and the falls are a velvety pink-plum flushed with magenta. This is a large, ruffled, beautifully proportioned flower that is sweetly scented.

Breeder: Schreiner, USA
Year of introduction: 1984
Flowering height: 3 feet (90cm)
Flowering period: Early to mid-season
Similar varieties: Jazzed Up

Superstition

Very few plants produce "black" flowers, and bearded irises are among the few. However, their numbers are limited, and like all "black"-flowered plants, they contain a tint of another hue. In reality, this one is a rich purple. In texture its falls are as glossy as silk taffeta, and its standards are silkier still. The beards are dark purple, and the whole flower is gently ruffled and heavily scented. The blooms are carried on strong stems above gray-green foliage to form a robust and healthy-looking plant. A truly handsome variety, it is ideal for areas in the garden that require a little drama.

Breeder: Schreiner, USA
Year of introduction: 1987
Flowering height: 3 feet (90cm)
Flowering period: Mid-season
Similar varieties: Before the Storm, Black Out, Interpol, Raven Hill, Swazi Princess

Beverly Sills

When it comes to the colors of garden flowers, pink must be one of the most popular. Sadly, however, pink varieties are the least robust of all bearded irises. Until the 1940's pink hybrids were almost nonexistent, and when they did appear they tended to be closer to lilac or peach than pink. This is because the pink pigmentation in bearded irises is not a dominant factor, so it is difficult to raise a truly pink variety. Nevertheless, this one—named after the well-known opera singer—is one of the best of its kind. Sweetly scented, the flowers are a soft, creamy coral-pink and have beards of the same tone and thick, frilly petals. The blooms are carried on short, strong stems and are produced in great profusion.

Breeder: Hager, USA
Year of introduction: 1979
Flowering height: 2½ feet (75cm)
Flowering period: Mid-season
Awards: DM (USA) 1985
Similar varieties: Anna Belle Babson, Jean Guymer, Playgirl, Vanity

Sweet Musette

This is a perfectly shaped modern iris. The flowers are large, heavily laced, and deeply serrated around the edges. The falls and standards are wide and flare outward to form a large, broad flower. Its falls are amethyst in color and the standards are a delicate washed contrast of soft pink. It has beards heavily tipped with bright orange, which adds an extra touch of color to the flowers. These sweetly scented blooms are carried on strong, straight stems well above the foliage. However, as with many varieties with large petals, the flowers can be damaged in poor weather. This iris, and others like it, should therefore be grown in a position that offers some protection against the elements.

Breeder: Schreiner, USA
Year of introduction: 1986
Flowering height: 3 feet (90cm)
Flowering period: Early to mid-season
Similar varieties: Afternoon Delight, Colette Thurillet

Song of Norway

Despite being an award winner, this beautiful variety may well cease to be grown in years to come. Although a truly handsome and robust plant, it lacks the extravagant ruffling so popular with iris fanciers today—in fact, the flowers contain almost no lacing or ruffling. In color they are the softest blue: so pale as to be almost white, with just a hint of lilac. On closer inspection, a faint trace of yellow can be detected in the background of the petals. The beards are very distinctive—so short and thick that they resemble little moustaches. The strongly perfumed flowers are borne on short, well-branched stems high above the foliage.

Breeder: Luihn, USA
Year of introduction: 1977
Flowering height: 4 feet (120cm)
Flowering period: Mid-season
Awards: DM (USA) 1986
Similar varieties: Babbling Brook, Codicil, Eleanor's Pride, Morwenna

Godfrey Owen

The world of the bearded iris is dominated by American hybrids. However, many outstanding varieties have also been bred in other countries. These sometimes fail to become widely distributed, remaining handsome secrets within their country of origin. This is one of them. Margaret Owen, the breeder of this attractive variety, named it after her late husband. In bright light, it has pale lemon standards and white falls that are edged with a broad band of lemon and carry bright yellow beards. The blooms are frilly, neatly ruffled, and borne in perfect symmetry on upright stems. The flowers have a strong lemon scent. Since this plant was bred in northern Europe, it is suitable for gardens that are not blessed with a great number of sunny days.

Breeder: Owen, UK
Year of introduction: 1986
Flowering height: 3 feet (90cm)
Flowering period: Mid-season
Similar varieties: Joyce Terry

Red Revival

Red is not a color found in wild irises since they contain too great a proportion of purple and brown pigments, which saturate any red that might be present in the petals. This variety is as close to red as any bearded iris will get. Its red-brown falls flare outward and each carries a contrasting beard surrounded by stripes. These are nicely complemented by caramel standards. Red Revival was one of the first varieties to be classed as a rebloomer. The ability to bloom for a second time is present in all types of bearded iris; however, more often than not it is the taller varieties that are selected for their second flush of flowers. The flowers produced later in the year are never as good as earlier blooms, although they are just as prolific and last for much longer. Miss Isabella Preston, the breeder of this variety, maintained an experimental garden in Ottawa, Canada.

Breeder: Preston, Canada
Year of introduction: 1975
Flowering height: 3 feet (90cm)
Flowering period: Early season and late summer to early fall
Similar varieties: Lady Friend, Warrior King

Oriental Glory

The blended colors of some bearded irises alter with the time of day and the weather. This is even more obvious if they are as vibrant as this variety. Essentially wine-red in color, the falls are heavily smeared with violet, which gives them their vibrancy. Each bright beard is surrounded by dollops of dusky pink. The falls are broad and evenly proportioned, while the standards are small and splay outward. The overall result is a lightly scented flower of dusky rose-violet, with a smooth and uncluttered outline. During the 1960's this plant was often used as a parent in the breeding of new hybrids. It was bred by Carl Salbach, a nurseryman from California.

Breeder: Salbach, USA
Year of introduction: 1952
Flowering height: 2½ feet (75cm)
Flowering period: Late season
Similar varieties: Flareup, Rancho Grande, Syncopation

Persian Berry

Look through the index of any gardening book containing a good number of bearded irises and you will see how wonderful their names are. Distinctly imaginative, they are unique within the horticultural world. As with the title of this variety, the rainbow colors of the blooms have inspired many. Unusual in tone, this variety has an uneven wash of what could be described as soft grape, light mulberry, or perhaps rosy lavender. It has narrow standards and broad falls, both with frilly edges. At either side of each orange beard sits a butterfly wing of deep, dusky pink. The lightly scented flowers are carried on straight stems to form a colorful, closely packed spike that rises from a robust plant. Larry Gaulter, who bred this variety, was by profession a painter and decorator.

Breeder: Gaulter, USA
Year of introduction: 1977
Flowering height: 2½ feet (75cm)
Flowering period: Mid-season
Similar varieties: Cranberry Ice, Good Looking

Jazz Festival

One of the newest varieties included in this book, this plant demonstrates just how far the bearded iris has developed over the past hundred years. It produces large, bicolored flowers with broad, heavily ruffled petals. The standards are soft buff-pink, while the horizontal falls are rose-violet and contain hints of maroon. Between the standards and the falls, and behind the beards, are distinctive style crests—an important part of the flower's reproductive system, connecting the ovary to the stigma. These are tan in color and look like small, winged petals. This flower is nicely scented, and its blooms are borne on upright stems with branching that is only apparent at the base.

Breeder: Schreiner, USA
Year of introduction: 1990
Flowering height: 41 inches (105cm)
Flowering period: Mid- to late season
Similar varieties: P.T. Barnum

Going My Way

With its thick, gently ruffled petals and lightly scented flowers, this older plicata iris is one of the most popular. Its standards are almost entirely purple, although the color is actually stippled and dotted over a white background. The falls are essentially white with a broad band of rich, dark purple around the edge. Despite its Californian origins, this reliable plant grows well in all climates.

Breeder: Gibson, USA
Year of introduction: 1972
Flowering height: 3 feet (90cm)
Flowering period: Mid- to late season
Similar varieties: Art Deco, Blue Staccato, Earl of Essex, Jesse's Song, Rare Treat, Stepping Out, Stitch in Time

Madeira Belle

White flowers are always popular, but in bearded irises they are seldom pure in color. Like modern wall paints, the petals often contain traces of another color—such as cream, blue, pink, or green—and this variety is an example of the phenomenon. White beards do give it some purity, but the blooms emerge from pale green buds. Ruffling was not found on the petals of bearded irises before 1963; since then, no variety has been introduced without it. These flowers are beautifully ruffled as well as lightly scented. They are carried on sturdy, well-branched stems, and the whole forms a short, very robust plant.

Breeder: Quadros, USA
Year of introduction: 1967
Flowering height: 2½ feet (75cm)
Flowering period: Late season
Similar varieties: Elizabeth Poldark, Rime Frost, Snowy Owl

War Sails

Once small and delicate, the flowers of the bearded iris are now twice the size of those introduced a hundred years ago. Often European in origin, the older plants could cope with the ravages of bad weather, unlike the big flowers of today, which are damaged by wind and rain. To overcome this, hybridizers have strengthened the flowers structurally by selecting varieties with extravagant ruffles and thick petals. In this variety we see it all. Ruffled to the extreme, the flowers are a luxurious, smooth, deep red-brown in color, with rich yellow beards that further enhance the red-brown color. The blooms are borne abundantly on a strong, straight main stem to form a handsome spike of flowers.

Breeder: Schreiner, USA
Year of introduction: 1984
Flowering height: 41 inches (105cm)
Flowering time: Mid-season
Similar varieties: Dutch Chocolate, Margrave, War Chief, Warrior King

Carnaby

When plants are described, some—like this variety, with its gentle blend of pinks—are often characterized as distinctly feminine. The flowers are nicely shaped, with peachy standards lightly flushed with lilac, and rose-purple falls broadly edged in the same color as the standards. With a very pale peach stripe down the center of each fall and soft orange beards, the whole flower has a sparkling sheen. Lightly scented, it has evenly proportioned, gently ruffled petals.

Breeder: Schreiner, USA
Year of introduction: 1973
Flowering height: 3 feet (90cm)
Flowering period: Mid-season
Similar varieties: Chinese Treasure, Festive Mood, Live Music

Jane Phillips

Pale irises are incredibly versatile, as they blend well with many other perennials. Of all the soft blue-lilac varieties grown today, this is still the most popular one in the UK. Distinctly old-fashioned, this classical iris has crepe-paper-like petals lined with veins of deeper color. The white beards sit on falls that hang gracefully downward. Some might consider this an unattractive trait, but when the blooms are fully open they form an elegant flower spike. The whole plant is disease resistant and very tough, with handsome gray-green leaves. As a parent plant, it is of historical importance. Many of its progeny, which includes Sapphire Hills (see page 37), are award-winning varieties. It was introduced by Dr. Robert Graves, who served as a doctor in World War I.

Breeder: Graves, USA
Year of introduction: 1950
Flowering height: 3 feet (90cm)
Flowering period: Mid-season
Similar varieties: Blue Rhythm, Derwentwater, Great Lakes, Harbor Blue

Annabel Jane

Brian Dodsworth, currently the most prolific breeder of Tall Bearded irises in the UK, named this elegant variety after his daughter. It is perhaps his finest achievement, producing heavily ruffled flowers of smooth lilac with short orange beards sitting on the falls. The flowers have a light, spicy scent and are borne in great profusion. They are poised perfectly on very tall stems above a clump of leaves that is exceptionally healthy. Despite being tall, this variety remains remarkably upright even on very windy days. It is excellent for placing at the back of a border among other perennials.

Breeder: Dodsworth, UK
Year of introduction: 1973
Flowering height: 41 inches (105cm)
Flowering period: Mid-season
Awards: DM (UK) 1977
Similar varieties: Mary Frances

Champagne Elegance

Some gardeners say bearded irises are not worth growing because their flowering season is so short. It may therefore come as a surprise to learn that there are hybrids that flower at least twice in one season. These are known as "remontant", or reblooming, varieties, and their flowering season varies around the world. In hotter areas, such as California, some will bloom all year round. In more temperate zones, such as northern Europe, they may bloom only twice: once in early summer, then again in late summer. Of the reblooming varieties, this is one of the finest. It has white standards and soft peachy falls. These flare out horizontally, and a ribbon of white runs around the edges. Each carries a beard of soft yellow. The flowers are frilly, small, and borne on sturdy stems above a short clump of leaves.

Breeder: Niswonger, USA
Year of introduction: 1987
Flowering height: 3 feet (90cm)
Flowering period: Early season, then again from late summer into early fall
Similar varieties: Coral Chalice, Magharee, Peach Spot

Lemon Brocade

An extremely laced and ruffled flower, this variety has petals of soft lemon-yellow. In shape they are typical of bearded irises introduced during the 1970's. The standards just touch at the top, forming a dome, while a beard of white, thickly stained with yellow sits on each of the gently arched falls. In front of each beard lies a large area of white. The petals are thick in substance, which helps the flower cope well with bad weather. Scented of lemons, this is a vigorous hybrid. It was introduced by Nat Rudolph, who normally specialized in the breeding of pink varieties.

Breeder: Rudolph, USA
Year of introduction: 1973
Flowering height: 2 feet (60cm)
Flowering period: Late season
Similar varieties: Eastertime, Joyce Terry

Queen In Calico

Over the years, Tall Bearded iris varieties have become quite daring in color. Traditional patterns and types, once serene and refined, are now sophisticated and exotic. The petals, previously small and smooth, now boast extravagant flounces and flares. In this variety we see these qualities stretched to the extreme. A plicata type, this iris has a deep cream base color, over which a dusky purple is splashed and speckled. The falls are additionally etched with purple lines and dots to such a degree that they resemble an Indian batik print. The beards are orange, and the flower has an unusual scent, reminiscent of chocolate. Sadly, in some countries, particularly those with a cooler climate, this is not a particularly robust plant. The fluted standards tend to splay open a little too much, allowing them to be damaged by severe weather.

Breeder: Gibson, USA
Year of introduction: 1980
Flowering height: 2½ feet (75cm)
Flowering period: Mid-season
Similar varieties: Caramba, Patina

Titan's Glory

The flowers of this vigorous variety are very large and flamboyantly ruffled. In color they are dark blue-purple. The petals are so shiny that the light positively bounces off them, and they are thick in substance, allowing the flower to remain perfect for at least three days, perhaps four. The falls carry deep blue-purple beards, which are so dark that they almost disappear. Each bloom is lightly scented and borne on a strong stem with widely spaced side branches. Like many varieties introduced during the latter years of the twentieth century, it has an excellent bud count, which means that the plant will remain in flower for many weeks.

Breeder: Schreiner, USA
Year of introduction: 1981
Flowering height: 3 feet (90cm)
Flowering period: Early to mid-season
Awards: DM (USA) 1988
Similar varieties: Larry Gaulter, Noble House, Temptone

Provençal

Like Schreiner's in Oregon, the Cayeux nursery in France is a family-run business now in its third generation. It has been raising irises for over seventy-five years. Located close to the banks of the Loire in central France, as breeders of irises they are well placed to raise plants that suit all areas of the world, from hot and sunny to damp and dull. This is a handsome variety with neatly shaped, plicata-type flowers. Its color, basically a rich red-maroon, is thickly speckled over a background of yellow. The beards are rich yellow and sit on large, round falls. The falls have a smooth outline with no trace of ruffling and a thick, silky texture. A robust variety, this plant has gray-green leaves and heavily scented flowers.

Breeder: Cayeux, France
Year of introduction: 1978
Flowering height: 3 feet (90cm)
Flowering period: Mid-season
Similar varieties: Kent Pride, Raspberry Fudge

Olympic Challenge

Until the middle of the twentieth century, no shade of orange existed within the rainbow repertoire of the bearded iris. Initially, those classed as orange were in reality peach or apricot; then, during the 1960's the first truly orange bearded irises emerged. These have never been robust—in cooler climates they do better in a hot summer—and even today, other colors produce plants with greater vigor. This variety—whose blooms are bright orange in strong sunlight—is more robust than most. The center of each fall is somewhat paler, and the falls flare out horizontally. Each fall carries a vivid orange beard. This iris is lightly scented, with a perfectly balanced shape.

Breeder: Schreiner, USA
Year of introduction: 1985
Flowering height: 41 inches (105cm)
Flowering time: Mid-season
Similar varieties: Deft Touch, Firebreather, Metaphor, Oktoberfest, Tangerine Sky

Out Yonder

Among the different types of Tall Bearded irises, the amoenas have interested breeders for many years, and as a consequence there are numerous varieties to choose from. This one is typical, with its pale standards and darker falls. The standards are lightly speckled at the base and flushed with deeper color, while the falls flare out horizontally and each carries a white beard with hairs touched with yellow. The flowers are slightly ruffled and carried on rigid stems with no side branching. In some varieties this can lead to flower spikes that look untidy, but in this one they remain elegant since each flower opens individually.

Breeder: Wickersham, USA
Year of introduction: 1969
Flowering height: 3 feet (90cm)
Flowering period: Mid- to late season
Similar varieties: Alizes, Best Bet, Conjuration, Mystique

Iris pallida

This is one of only two Tall Bearded iris species in existence. It originated in southern Europe, and for centuries its roots were used in medicines, cosmetics, and toothpaste, and—in some areas of Italy—to flavor wine! By the eighteenth century it was included in ornamental borders and later still was used, along with *I. variegata*, to breed new varieties. As a result, this is the ancestor of all bearded irises. From papery bracts, small buds unpeel into delicate, lilac-blue flowers with translucent petals. The flowers are small and traditional in shape, exceptionally fragrant, and carried on tall, very slender stems above handsome gray-green leaves. As a garden plant it is robust and will cope with the competition of other perennials.

Breeder: Species iris
Flowering height: 3 feet (90cm)
Flowering time: Early season
Similar varieties: *I. pallida* var. *dalmatica*, *I. pallida* 'Variegata', *I. pallida* 'Argentea Variegata'

Dusky Challenger

Black flowers are unusual. When they do occur, they are never truly black but always a deep shade of brown, purple, or blue. At the time of its introduction, this was one of the darkest irises ever seen. Best described as purple-black, its flowers are large and nicely ruffled. It has shiny petals, a quality found in very few plants and present only in those with thick petals. On each fall sits an almost matching beard. The heavy, sharp fragrance is unusual and reminiscent of hot chocolate. The flowers are borne on strong stems and form a perfectly balanced spike, making this an excellent border plant.

Breeder: Schreiner, USA
Year of introduction: 1986
Flowering height: 3 feet (90cm)
Flowering period: Mid- to late season
Awards: DM (USA) 1992, Premio Firenze 1989
Similar varieties: Barry Gaulter, Best Bet

Sapphire Hills

A truly blue-blooded variety, this comes from a long line of award-winning parents. It is a perfect example of how, by crossing the best varieties around, another beautiful variety can be bred. When it comes to breeding new plants, hybridizers generally know exactly what they are aiming for. This variety was introduced during the early 1970's, at a time when there were many mid-blue bearded irises available. However, most did not have unruffled petals. Sapphire Hills came from a crossbreeding of the most beautiful mid-blue varieties with the best of the ruffled ones. The spikes are perfectly balanced with gently ruffled flowers. On closer inspection, each petal is rendered shiny with what looks like a fine net of crystals. Flaring falls carry white beards that are tipped yellow toward the back.

Breeder: Schreiner, USA
Year of introduction: 1971
Flowering height: 3 feet (90cm)
Flowering period: Mid-season
Similar varieties: Breakers, Full Reward, Yaquina Blue

Skier's Delight

There are dozens of white bearded irises to choose from. Almost all are excellent, and selecting a favorite can be extremely difficult. Occasionally, however, a variety will stand out—and this is one of them. Its flowers are ruffled, laced, and lightly scented, and the white beards carry a dab of yellow. The petals are etched with hairline veins that make the flowers just about translucent. These are borne on very straight stems with almost no side branches. In some varieties this can be a disadvantage, but in this hybrid the flowers open one at a time and the resulting flower spike is one of immense poise that produces a lot of buds. It is excellent even on rainy days.

Breeder: Schreiner, USA
Year of introduction: 1982
Flowering height: 2½ feet (75cm)
Flowering period: Late season
Similar varieties: America's Cup, Immortality, Laced Cotton, Leda's Lover

Starshine

A chameleon of a flower, this variety could be described as white or yellow. The standards, upon opening, are white with a flush of soft, buff yellow in the center. The falls, as they unpeel, are white flushed with violet, and each carries a yellow beard, surrounded by heavy veins of ocher. As they age, the flowers lose their bright coloration, fading to almost white. This vigorous, sweetly scented variety was bred by Jesse Wills of Nashville, Tennessee. Wills was president of the American Iris Society from 1943 to 1946. At the time of its introduction, and for years later, this iris was much admired for its smooth, tailored flowers.

Breeder: Wills, USA
Year of introduction: 1949
Flowering height: 41 inches (105cm)
Flowering period: Mid-season
Similar varieties: Goodwill Messenger, Green Prophecy

Susan Bliss

Arthur J. Bliss bred this variety during his retirement. William R. Dykes, then secretary of the Royal Horticultural Society in the UK, was sorting out the botanical classification of irises, and gave Bliss two collected forms of species iris—*Iris pallida* and *I. variegata*. The aim was to check their identification by crossing them. This could well be one of the offspring. Pure lilac, its delicate flowers are small, with creped standards and smooth falls. The small beards are tipped red and surrounded by white stripes. The flowers have a strong, spicy fragrance and are borne on slender stems above short, gray-green leaves. This iris is an example of how, over the years, the names of garden plants can get confused. It was sold to me as Susan Bliss, but according to a photograph in an American Society Bulletin of 1970, Susan Bliss should have paler standards and darker falls!

Breeder: Bliss, UK
Year of introduction: 1922
Flowering height: 2½ feet (75cm)
Flowering period: Mid-season
Similar varieties: *I. pallida*

White City

On opening, the flowers of this much-respected variety are pale blue, fading over time to almost white. It has white beards tipped with yellow that are surrounded by tan-brown veins. This was one of the first varieties to have falls flaring outward rather than hanging down like the ears of a dog. The petals are generally smooth, although the falls curl around the edges and the standards are crinkled rather than ruffled. Small in size, the unscented blooms are carried on long, slender stems to form a tough and reliable plant. This variety was bred by Olive Murrell, who managed her English nursery at Orpington in Kent single-handed following the death of her husband. Over a number of years she introduced many seedlings that at the time were very popular, but sadly this is one of the few varieties to remain in commercial horticulture.

Breeder: Murrell, UK
Year of introduction: 1939
Flowering time: Mid-season
Flowering height: 41 inches (105cm)
Awards: DM (UK) 1940
Similar varieties: Cup Race, Laced Cotton

Snow Mound

An appropriately named hybrid, this plant produces a great many flowers that, as its name suggests, form a mound of color. The blooms are delicately scented and lightly ruffled, with pale standards that fade to almost white over time. The falls are purple and these also fade, gaining a pale violet edging. On each fall sits a yellow-tipped beard surrounded by white and brown veins. Although it is a vigorous plant with strong, upright stems, as with many varieties that produce a lot of flowers, the stems are inclined to fall over in windy weather. In exposed gardens it might therefore be necessary to stake the plants.

Breeder: Schreiner, USA
Year of introduction: 1976
Flowering height: 3 feet (90cm)
Flowering period: Early season
Similar varieties: Gay Parasol, Margarita, Proud Tradition, Sweet Reflections

Staten Island

Many irises that were once popular are still grown in gardens for their beauty and vigor, but their names have long been forgotten. This is one of those, often grown but seldom named. When first introduced, it was a landmark variety, much respected for the sharp contrast in color between its standards and falls. The standards are velvety and bright yellow, while the falls are rich maroon-red. On each fall sits a yellow beard surrounded by yellow stripes. The falls flare gently outward, while the standards touch neatly at the top, to create finely shaped blooms without any ruffling. The flowers are sweetly scented and emerge from slender, pointed buds on slim, sturdy stems.

Breeder: Smith, USA
Year of introduction: 1945
Flowering height: 41 inches (105cm)
Flowering time: Mid-season
Similar varieties: High Command, Rajah, Supreme Sultan

Caliente

The flowers of the bearded iris, once small and smoothly shaped, have seen many changes over the past twenty years. However, many gardeners do not care for the newer, more flamboyant style of flower. When planted in a mixed border the large, ruffled flowers of today's bearded irises can take the attention away from more delicate blooms. In style, this variety is halfway between the old and the new. Its rich red-brown flowers are gently ruffled and reasonably large. The falls are rounded, poised horizontally to the standards, and have a silky texture. The short, burnt-orange beards accentuate the color of the petals. A robust variety, it carries its scented blooms on sturdy but not thick stems, well above a clump of healthy gray-green leaves.

Breeder: Luihn, USA
Year of introduction: 1967
Flowering height: 3 feet (90cm)
Flowering period: Mid-season
Similar varieties: Tall Chief

Wabash

Although not dramatic by modern standards, this elegant old variety was a landmark in the breeding of bearded irises. Varieties like these are not easy to breed, partly because they are so far removed from their wild parents. This one has white standards and royal-purple falls, the edges of which are narrowly banded with white. Each fall carries a yellow beard surrounded by short white stripes. The blooms are small and lightly scented, with rounded falls and taller, wavy standards. The standards are carried on widely branched, very tall stems. Like many older varieties, this one produces very few flowers on each branch, but it is a tough and reliable garden plant.

Breeder: Williamson, USA
Year of introduction: 1936
Flowering height: 41 inches (105cm)
Flowering period: Mid-season
Awards: DM (USA) 1940
Similar varieties: Bal Masqué, Snow Mound, Sweet Reflections

Ola Kala

Yellow is a color natural to the wild parents of bearded irises, so yellow flowers are easy to breed and many have been introduced. Despite this, the older yellow varieties are still as good as many modern ones. This flower was bred by Jacob Sass, who with his brother Hans emigrated from Germany to Nebraska in 1884. The brothers introduced a great number of varieties, many of which are of historical importance. This is a good example and is typical of its time. The bright yellow flowers are smoothly shaped but small in size, so much of the plant's energy goes into producing a robust clump. In addition, as the flowers are small, they do not collapse in windy conditions.

Breeder: Sass, USA
Year of introduction: 1941
Flowering height: 41 inches (105cm)
Flowering period: Late season
Awards: DM (USA) 1948
Similar varieties: Buttercup Bower, Golden Encore

Edith Wolford

At the time this variety was introduced, it was truly original and very unusual. Since then, many similar varieties have followed. The standards are very pale yellow, with contrasting soft violet-blue falls. The edges of the petals are paler in color, and the short beards are pale orange. The flowers are large, square in shape, and extremely ruffled. These are borne on sturdy stems which remain respectably upright in even the worst weather. Placing this variety in a garden border can present some problems, especially if the border includes other plants in gentle colors. It is perhaps best grown among other irises that contain the same colors—yellow and blue.

Breeder: Schreiner, USA
Year of introduction: 1986
Flowering height: 2½ feet (75cm)
Flowering period: Mid-season
Awards: DM (USA) 1993
Similar varieties: Betty Simon, Gladys Austin, Jurassic Park

Iris germanica 'Amas'

Despite being a rather dull and old-fashioned flower, this is the ancestor of almost all Tall Bearded irises. Discovered by missionaries in central Europe, it was given to the English plantsman Sir Michael Foster. He named it after the district in which it was found, then used it to cross with other bearded irises. This resulted in varieties with larger flowers than others of the day. Whether Foster knew this or not, the consequence was that all varieties to follow produced larger blooms. The standards of this flower are dull purple, and the falls a darker purple with white beards surrounded by stripes. The falls are floppy, resembling the ears of a dog, and the standards are flimsy and liable to splay open. However, this remarkably tough plant will thrive in either partial shade or full sun and, unlike many irises today, will bloom even if not frequently divided.

Breeder: Collected form of *I. germanica*
Year of introduction: 1885
Flowering height: 3 feet (90cm)
Flowering period: Early season
Similar varieties: *I. germanica*,
I. germanica 'The King'

Blenheim Royal

Of the thousands of Tall Bearded iris varieties introduced over the past sixty years, many are so similar that only an iris enthusiast can tell them apart. This is particularly true when it comes to dark blue and blue-purple varieties. Those that do remain popular have everything—pure color, thick petals, and large, ruffled flowers—and Blenheim Royal is one of these. A robust and reliable garden variety, it produces evenly proportioned, rich blue-purple flowers, with extravagantly ruffled petals that are thick in substance. The falls flare outward horizontally and a dense beard sits on each. It is a lightly scented variety, and its flowers are carried on strong stems.

Breeder: Schreiner, USA
Year of introduction: 1990
Flowering height: 3 feet (90cm)
Flowering period: Mid-season
Similar varieties: Breakers, Honky Tonk Blues, Pledge Allegiance

Silverado

Some varieties are so important historically in the development of the bearded iris that no self-respecting collector should be without them. Introduced by Schreiner's in Oregon, this is just one of the many hundreds of varieties bred by this nursery since its foundation in 1935. Schreiner's work has been so important that all iris catalogs around the world list at least one of their hybrids. The petals of this pale iris are lightly touched with purple, gently ruffled, and covered by an enchanting, glistening sheen of silver. It has short, white beards that are only just visible. The flowers are scented and carried on strong, sturdy stems above the gray-green leaves.

Breeder: Schreiner, USA
Year of introduction: 1984
Flowering height: 3 feet (90cm)
Flowering period: Mid-season
Awards: DM (USA) 1994
Similar varieties: Olympiad, Pacific Mist

Ringo

The flowers of this robust plant are large, perfectly proportioned, ruffled, and heavily scented. The falls flare out horizontally and are darker than the standards. Each fall carries an orange beard and is edged with a band of white. The blooms are held on strong stems, but since these do not bear many side branches, the flowering period is rather short. At one time breeders raised varieties purely for show stands, and to display the flowers at their best, they required straight stems that produced only a few side branches. Since this variety was introduced, many similar hybrids have followed that bloom for longer. However, the flower quality of this one has yet to be beaten.

Breeder: Shoop, USA
Year of introduction: 1979
Flowering height: 3 feet (90cm)
Flowering period: Mid-season
Similar varieties: Navajo Blanket, Sweeter Than Wine

Rosette Wine

This is not a common color. Vivid in shade, it is best described as rosy purple. The underside of the falls are suffused with very pale caramel, while the beards are pale blue. Blue beards like this are more commonly found on smaller bearded irises. They not only add extra color to the falls, but also increase the individuality of each variety. Thoroughly modern in shape, the petals are extremely ruffled, fluted, and very silky. A scented hybrid, the plant produces long side branches. These hold the flowers well away from a strong main stem to create a beautifully proportioned flower spike. A truly handsome plant, it remains upright even in windy and wet conditions.

Breeder: Schreiner, USA
Year of introduction: 1989
Flowering height: 3 feet (90cm)
Flowering period: Mid-season
Similar varieties: Gypsy Romance, Thriller

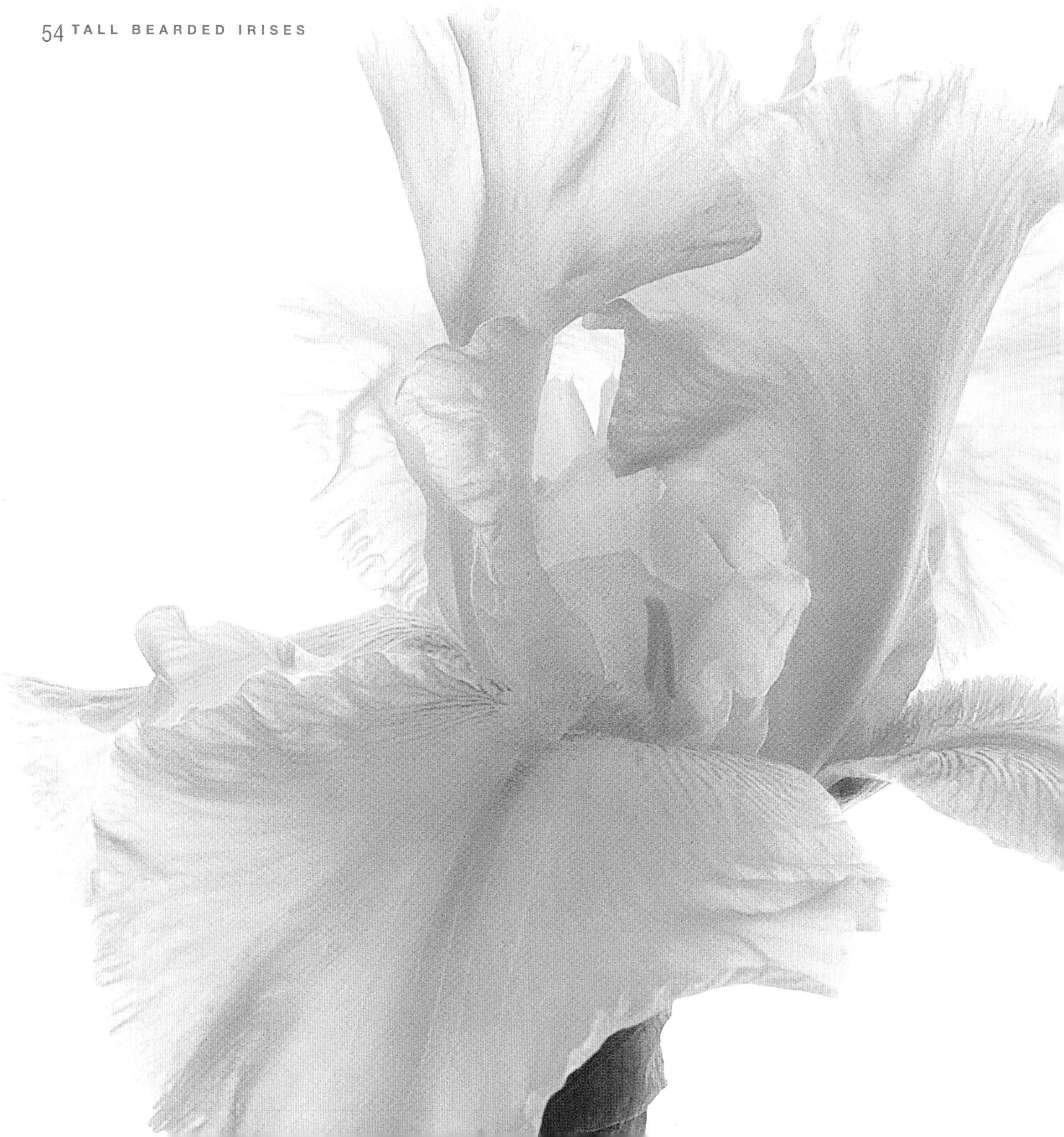

Jeanne Price

Self-colored flowers are usually extremely easy to blend into a mixed border. Yellow, however, is not a color that suits all styles of gardening, and in the gentle, temperate gardens of northern Europe it can look brash and demanding. Nevertheless, this yellow variety is perfect for planting in drifts since it is easy to grow and quick to multiply. Its flowers are a handsome color. Each bloom is gently ruffled and delicately pinched around the edges. It has a strong but somewhat sickly scent.

Breeder: B. Jones, USA
Year of introduction: 1977
Flowering height: 3 feet (90cm)
Flowering period: Mid- to late season
Similar varieties: Country Gold, Helen Boehm, Tut's Gold

Olympic Torch

This is a distinctive, sweetly scented, rich golden bronze iris. On closer inspection it seems to contain different layers of color, with its orange smeared over a background of yellow. Its standards curve gently inward, just touching at the top, and the falls arch downward and are very slightly ruffled. The only break in color comes from zebra stripes of brown on either side of the yellow-bronze beards. Stripes like these were present in nearly all iris hybrids before the 1980's—today, they are almost nonexistent. Sadly, like many older hybrids, this plant is not generous with the number of flowers it produces.

Breeder: Schreiner, USA
Year of introduction: 1956
Flowering height: 41 inches (105cm)
Flowering period: Late season
Similar varieties: Brindisi, Cable Car

median
bearded irises

The category known as Median irises evolved only fifty years ago. Before this time, the types that mainly flowered earlier than the Tall Bearded hybrids were simply unclassified. Seen as the runts of Tall Bearded varieties or sometimes as variations of wild iris, this is a confusing group. It came about as hybridizers began to purposefully cross irises of differing sizes and flowering times. The resulting plants required some distinctive classification in order to be fully recognized. These plants are perhaps even more varied in form, height, and color than their Tall Bearded relatives, and in many ways they make better garden plants.

Serenity Prayer

Type: SDB

Initially, the Standard Bearded category of irises was called "Lilliputs," a wonderful title for this particular robust little plant. It produces very neat flowers that are excellent in quality. In color these are milky white, scented, and freely produced. The standards are round, while the falls flare out like the propellers of a helicopter. The falls are petite in size and each carries a bright lilac blue beard that is highlighted on the shoulders with patches of yellow. As with all Standard Dwarf Bearded irises, the flowers just skim the top of the leaves. Since it is a newer introduction, the length of bloom is long, when compared to older varieties: the flowers will easily last for three weeks.

Breeder: Dyer, USA
Year of introduction: 1989
Flowering height: 13 inches (32cm)
Flowering period: Late spring
Similar varieties: Blue Line

Ruby Chimes

Type: IB

The dark red varieties of Median irises in nature are particularly luxurious when compared to those of the Tall Bearded hybrids. This is a good example. Rich deep red in color, the petals are thick in substance and have a velvety texture. In shape they are similar to those of the taller hybrids, but their size is well in proportion to the height of the stems. The blooms emit a spicy fragrance and are produced in profusion. This variety, like all the members of this group, is excellent as a border plant. The foliage, which is wide and mid green, adds extra structure to a border of mixed perennials.

Breeder: Brown, USA
Year of introduction: 1971
Flowering height: 2 feet (60cm)
Flowering period: Late spring to early summer
Similar varieties: Red Zinger

Iris variegata

Type: MTB

I defy anyone not to be enchanted by this iris. Historically important, it is one of only two wild types. As a parent it is responsible for almost all yellow-flowered Tall Bearded irises. Now categorized as a Miniature Tall Bearded iris— also known as Table Irises in the United States—it originates from northern Europe, where it was once found in every garden. Frequently grown because it is both reliable and tough, it is still a marvelous garden plant. The small, delicate flowers have rounded petals that are translucent in substance. The standards are lemon yellow, while the falls are white, heavily patterned with fine maroon veins, and edged with a rim of lemon. The blooms are borne on short, slender stems just above the top of its foliage.

Breeder: species iris
Flowering height: 2 feet (60cm)
Flowering period: Late spring to early summer
Similar varieties: Bumblebee Delight

Sherbet Lemon

Type: IB

A truly handsome and prolific variety, this is a perfect Median Bearded iris. Its flowers are borne on upright stems over a good number of weeks. Although many blooms are carried on each stem, these never become squashed as they open. In a border these plants are wonderful for adding early summer color. The tone of the flowers is pure, and the translucent petals are clear yellow. The standards are paler in tone than the falls, on which sit beards of lemon-yellow. In form the petals are rounded and ruffled, and as with all Median Bearded irises, these will not suffer in bad weather. This iris is especially useful for gardens in less hospitable climates.

Breeder: Bartlett, UK
Year of introduction: 1991
Flowering height: 20 inches (50cm)
Flowering period: Late spring to early summer
Similar varieties: Lemon Pop, Maui Moonlight

Curlew

Type: BB

Until the mid-twentieth century, many hybridizers aiming for taller plants found that their progeny were too small to be classed as Tall Bearded irises, so the category of Border Bearded irises was created. Time and again, the name of John Taylor comes up as a breeder of Standard Dwarf Bearded irises; however, the few taller varieties he introduced are still among the best around. The blooms of this heavily scented plant are a lovely yellow. Its standards are pure in color and just touch at the top to create a rounded, domed shape. The falls arch gently downward, and in bright light, a flash of white can be seen sitting in front of the yellow beards. Each bloom emerges just above a lush clump of broad, mid-green leaves, and the flowers are produced in great quantity for weeks.

Breeder: Taylor, UK
Year of introduction: 1967
Flowering height: 2 feet (60cm)
Flowering period: Late spring to early summer
Similar varieties: Mostest

Iris flavescens

Type: IB

This extremely vigorous plant produces delicate flowers with lemon standards. These open out to advertise themselves to the pollinating abilities of passing bees. Varieties with standards like these would normally be damaged by windy and wet weather, but not this one. Instead, the open standards allow the large, jagged-edge-style arms to poke through, adding to the plant's character. The falls are cream and decorated at each side of the yellow beard with veins of brown. Probably a hybrid of *I. pallida* and *I. variegata*, its survival over the years is testimony to its robustness as a garden plant. The blooms are borne on rigid stems from side branches that each produce up to three flowers during the flowering period. Although unscented, this is a valuable plant for growing in a border, as it will thrive among even the most competitive of perennials.

Breeder: de Candolle, Switzerland
Year of introduction: 1813
Flowering height: 2½ feet (75cm)
Flowering period: Late spring to early summer

Shampoo

Type: IB

The colors of Tall Bearded irises tend to be clean and clear, but the flowers of many smaller varieties can be quite different. In this variety we see just how far from nature the colors of some flowers have strayed. Its blooms are essentially bronze, with the falls slightly deeper in color. These flare outward horizontally and are gently waved around the edges. They carry self-colored beards. The standards are ruffled and domed in shape. When included in a planting scheme, this variety needs to be among flowers that are similar in color, such as lady's mantle (*Alchemilla mollis*).

Breeder: Messick, USA
Year of introduction: 1975
Flowering height: 1½ feet (45cm)
Flowering period: Late spring to early summer
Similar varieties: Tan Tingo

Bronzaire

Type: IB

Because they are smaller, the flowers of Median Bearded irises often need to be more dramatic in color than those of varieties with larger flowers. The color here is both unique and luxurious. Bred in Somerset by Cy Bartlett, the UK's foremost breeder of smaller irises, this hybrid is just one of the many he has introduced. It is a particularly fine example, with golden-bronze flowers that are larger than many of its type. The standards are a smooth golden yellow and ruffled, while the velvety falls have gently wavy edges and are more bronze in color. On each sits a thick, bushy beard of the same color. The flowers are carried on stems that produce at least four blooms at a time, above very healthy foliage.

Breeder: Bartlett, UK
Year of introduction: 1991
Flowering height: 20 inches (50cm)
Flowering period: Late spring to early summer
Similar varieties: Discovered Gold

Gingerbread Man

Type: SDB

Of all the Median Bearded irises, the Standard Dwarf Bearded types produce the greatest number of varieties, in the widest range of colors. Their flowers are quite distinctive in form, with domed standards and horizontal falls. Since these plants are low growing and in a border they are viewed from above, both the color and shape of the falls are of great importance. If the falls arched downward, the whole shape, plus the dramatic color of the flower, would be lost. This variety demonstrates excellently why the falls need to flare out. Its soft brown standards are delicately ruffled and washed with purple toward the base. Its falls are darker in color, smooth in texture, and shaped like propellers. In stark contrast, sitting on them are neat beards of lilac.

Breeder: Jones, USA
Year of introduction: 1969
Flowering height: 10 inches (25cm)
Flowering period: Late spring

Eye Bright

Type: SDB

I well remember John Taylor. A tall and distinguished gentleman, he was always handsomely dressed. When he died, he left behind a legacy of beautiful irises, many of which are still sold throughout the world. His career in the breeding of bearded irises began when he bought a packet of seed from Olive Murrell's Orpington Nurseries in Kent, England. This whim started him breeding his own plants and resulted in hundreds of new hybrids. This variety is one of his finest, producing a mass of bright yellow flowers. The long falls curl up around the edges and on these are etched maroon stripes that bear a distinct resemblance to eyelashes.

Breeder: Taylor, UK
Year of introduction: 1977
Flowering height: 1 foot (30cm)
Flowering period: Late spring
Similar varieties: Ace of Clubs, Eye Magic, Sun Doll

Melon Honey

Type: SDB

Orange flowers emerged earlier in the development of the Standard Dwarf Bearded iris than in the Tall Bearded hybrids. As with the taller irises, however, their color is seldom pure. The petite flowers of this variety are soft orange, resembling the flesh of a cantaloupe. The standards touch at the top to form a gentle dome, and below these the falls flare outward, each carrying a white flush that sits just in front of an orange beard. So many flowers are produced that they tend to mound over one another, which from a distance is extremely effective.

Breeder: Roberts, USA
Year of introduction: 1972
Flowering height: 1 foot (30cm)
Flowering period: Late spring
Similar varieties: Orange Caper, Orange Tiger

Hot Spice

Type: IB

Many hybridizers become involved in the iris society of their home country. At the time of writing, Terry Aitken, the breeder of this handsome variety, is the editor of the Bulletin of the American Iris Society. These societies, made up of enthusiasts and those who make a living from the flower, are generous with their passion and do much to share their knowledge with others. This excellent plant has plicata-type flowers that are thick in substance. Essentially a chocolate-brown, the color is speckled and dotted over a background of rich yellow. The flowers are frilly with horizontal, flaring falls.

Breeder: Aitken, USA
Year of introduction: 1989
Flowering height: 2 feet (60cm)
Flowering period: Late spring to early summer
Similar varieties: Butter Pecan, Golden Muffin, Hot Fudge

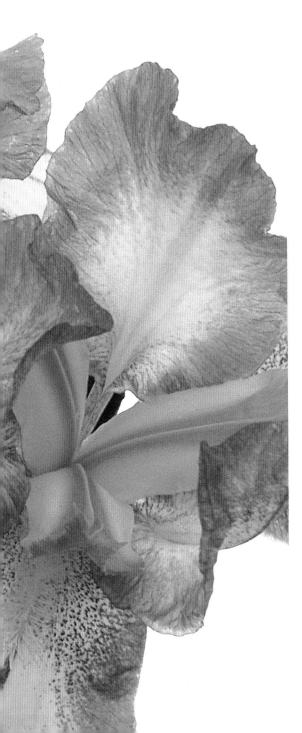

Raspberry Acres

Type: IB

An extremely prolific plant, this variety is an excellent example of how robust these smaller types can be. The flowers are plicata in type, featuring a white background that is edged with a neatly stitched band of pale violet-rose. The falls have a narrower edging. Lightly but unusually scented, the blooms are borne just above the foliage for many weeks. This is an excellent border plant that, since it is vigorous, will not be intimidated by the lustier garden perennials such as hardy geraniums. It was bred by Wilma Greenlee: it is interesting to note that, unlike in the world of rose breeding, women are as prominent as men as breeders of new bearded irises.

Breeder: Greenlee, USA
Year of introduction: 1968
Flowering height: 2 feet (60cm)
Flowering period: Late spring to early summer
Similar varieties: Light Laughter

Jungle Shadows

Type: IB

Although this is perhaps not the most beautiful of flowers, I challenge anyone to dream up a more sinister color combination. A favorite since its introduction, nothing quite like it has appeared since. Aptly named, the standards are a mixture of dull purple and brown, flecked and stained over the petals and around the edges. Inside, they are heavily flushed with purple. The falls are similar in color to the standards, but overlaid with deeper tones of brown. Unfortunately, the flowers are unscented. Raised by Sass, this variety was introduced after his death.

Breeder: Sass, USA
Year of introduction: 1959
Flowering height: 20 inches (50cm)
Flowering period: Late spring to early summer

Az Ap

Type: IB

The Intermediate Bearded iris is so called because its flowering season is between those of the dwarf varieties and the taller ones. This is an excellent example of its type, with blooms produced prolifically on upright stems that, unlike in Standard Dwarf varieties, are branched. As the extra branching means more blooms, the flowering period is longer than for this iris's smaller sisters. The flowers of this variety appear to be of a single color, but are veined with a darker shade. In bright sun, this darker shade can be seen edging the petals, which are rounded with delicately closed standards and flaring falls each carrying a beard of mid blue.

Breeder: Ensminger, USA
Year of introduction: 1980
Flowering height: 1½ feet (45cm)
Flowering period: Late spring to early summer
Similar varieties: Bel Azure, Bedtime Story, Hellcat

Happy Mood

Type: IB

The early Intermediate varieties were the result of the crossing of Standard Dwarf Bearded hybrids with Tall Bearded irises. The flowers are usually tough, and the plants are excellent in borders. They are ideal in between small and tall later-flowering varieties. Some, like this one, are not blessed with a tremendous amount of flowers, but those blooms that do emerge are certainly pretty. These are soft lilac in color and plicata in type. The color is strongly spotted and veined over a background of white, and the standards are almost entirely lilac. The petal edges are quietly wavy, while the falls droop gently to highlight their rounded shape. On each fall sits a white beard tipped with yellow.

Breeder: Brown, USA
Year of introduction: 1967
Flowering height: 2 feet (60cm)
Flowering period: Late spring to early summer
Similar varieties: Levity

Blue Hendred

Type: SDB

A delightful little variety, this plant produces a mass of daintily shaped sky-blue flowers—in dwarf irises, blue flowers are truer in color than those of their taller relatives. This variety has falls that flick outward horizontally, curling slightly around the edges. Its standards, also gently ruffled, curve inward to form a dome. All Standard Dwarf Bearded irises produce flowers that are 2–3 inches (5–7cm) across. This is no exception, and as with many of its relatives, the blooms emerge from a mass of spiky leaves to form a colorful mound. A prettily colored variety, with white beards, it is an excellent companion to early-flowering perennials such as pulmonarias.

Breeder: Watkins, UK
Year of introduction: 1969
Flowering height: 1 foot (30cm)
Flowering period: Late spring
Similar varieties: Austrian Sky, Bedford Lilac, Blue Denim, Tinkerbell

Sarah Taylor

Type: SDB

This is yet another delightful little iris from English hybridizer John Taylor. Its wavy, creamy-yellow petals are thick in substance and paler around the edges. Each fall has a central stripe etched into it and features a starkly contrasting beard of violet-blue. Like all Standard Dwarf Bearded irises, this is a particularly tough plant and once happy will form a thick, leafy clump that survives extremely well in a border among other perennials. However, in common with other varieties, when first planted it may take a little time to settle in.

Breeder: Taylor, UK
Year of introduction: 1979
Flowering height: 9 inches (23cm)
Flowering period: Late spring
Similar varieties: Kayo, Kentucky Blue Grass

Meadow Court

Type: BB

The iris world is very close knit, and nowhere more so than among the breeders of Median Bearded irises. When founded, this category soon became the talking point of hybridizers around the world. British and American breeders communicated readily about what they had achieved and what could be done, passing plants and ideas among themselves. Many came from families who had already established themselves as hybridizers of irises. Neel, the breeder of this variety, married the daughter of Olive Murrell, a well-known British iris breeder. Aftre she died, Neel took over the running of Murrell's nursery in Kent. Because of its robust constitution, this variety is a favorite with growers. It produces large ruffled flowers with yellow standards and fluted, yellow-edged falls with maroon centers.

Breeder: Neel, UK
Year of introduction: 1965
Flowering height: 1½ feet (45cm)
Flowering period: Late spring to early summer

Brown Lasso

Type: BB

Much admired at the time of its introduction, this is the only Median Bearded iris to have been awarded the Dykes Medal. A heavily scented bloom, it has extremely unusual coloring. The falls are violet, flare outward horizontally, and are widely edged with a band of caramel. The standards are yellow, flushed at the base with butterscotch. The complete flower is very ruffled and square in form. Each bloom is borne on a sturdy stem that carries four well-spaced branches. Over its blooming period this prolific variety produces at least three flowers on each branch.

Breeder: Buckles, introduced after his death by Niswonger, USA
Year of introduction: 1975
Flowering height: 22 inches (55cm)
Flowering period: Late spring to early summer
Awards: DM (USA) 1981

Just Jennifer

Type: BB

Before the birth of the Border Bearded category, all irises less than 2½ feet (75cm) tall were classed as Intermediates. However, some flowered at the same time as the Tall Bearded irises, so a section was introduced with a title that suggested that its varieties would make good border plants. The first hybrid was listed under this section in 1950. As a hybridizer, John Taylor worked for some time to achieve a good white Median Bearded iris—this variety is a fitting climax to his work. Even the beards are white. The petals are very ruffled, evenly proportioned, and translucent , while the falls flare outward below short, wide standards.

Breeder: Taylor, UK
Year of introduction: 1983
Flowering height: 22 inches (55cm)
Flowering period: Late spring to early summer
Similar varieties: Early Frost, Low Ho Silver

Lilli-White

Type: SDB

Truly mongrel in parentage, this old variety is still popular. It is the result of the cross of a white form of *I. lutescens*, the original dwarf species iris of gardens, with a Tall Bearded seedling that itself was never introduced. It is often the case that crosses will produce a plant that is not good enough to introduce, but nevertheless contains some quality valuable enough to pass on. The cross of these two oddballs resulted in a white flower that matches any introduced in recent years. Its petals are almost translucent, and the beards are immaculately white. The flowers are gently ruffled and produced in vast quantities. Walter Welch, the breeder of this delightful plant, was an artist and interior decorator who acquired his first irises from the breeder of Green Spot, Paul Cook.

Breeder: Welch, USA
Year of introduction: 1957
Flowering height: 10 inches (25cm)
Flowering period: Late spring
Similar varieties: Apollo's Touch, Bibury, Cotton Blossom, Zero

Dark Spark

Type: SDB

This bold example of a Standard Dwarf Bearded iris has deep purple flowers whose falls feature purple-black patches that are just about visible and sit on the petals like dark, velvety pools. In these patches sit purple beards touched with ginger toward the back. The falls splay outward, while the ruffled, shiny standards curl over one another to form a neat dome. These bright little flowers bloom at the same height as their foliage.

Breeder: Sindt, USA
Year of introduction: 1967
Flowering height: 10 inches (25cm)
Flowering period: Late spring
Similar varieties: Banbury Ruffles, Dark Vader, Little Shadow, Michael Paul

Bold Print

Type: IB

The 4-inch (10-cm) blooms of this Californian variety are typical of those of Intermediate hybrids. The standards and falls are round and evenly proportioned. In color, they are plicata in type. Basically white, the falls are neatly stitched with purple. This stitching extends to the standards and is found around the edges, with a further wash of purple smeared over them. A free-flowering variety, the plant carries its blooms on strong, upright, well-branched stems.

Breeder: Gatty, USA
Year of introduction: 1981
Flowering height: 22 inches (55cm)
Flowering period: Late spring to early summer
Similar varieties: Arctic Fancy, Batik, Cee Jay, Rare Edition

Sapphire Gem

Type: SDB

This delightful little variety produces flowers that are small in size, with round petals that are gently waved along the edge. The falls flare outward rigidly and are smeared with a tint of light purple. On these sit white beards. The blooms are produced evenly and in great quantity, and—as with all good Standard Dwarf Bearded irises— the plant forms a neat cushion of flowers. Like others in the group, it can be grown either as an edging plant or in front of taller varieties to extend the bearded iris flowering season.

Breeder: Schmelzer, USA
Year of introduction: 1976
Flowering height: 14 inches (35cm)
Flowering period: Late spring
Similar varieties: Rain Dance, Sapphire Jewels

Little Blackfoot

Type: SDB

This attractive little plant could be considered somewhat old-fashioned by today's standards, but it demonstrates beautifully the difference between the Standard Dwarf and the Tall Bearded irises. The flowers are small by comparison with those of the Tall Bearded irises, but they are in perfect proportion to the length of the stems. This rich purple variety has falls that are small and velvety, and sit acutely horizontal below the round, neatly domed standards. The beards are soft blue.

Breeder: Reinhardt
Year of introduction: 1967
Flowering height: 15 inches (37cm)
Flowering period: Late spring
Similar varieties: Jewel Baby, Little Black Belt, Well Suited

bearded irises
in the garden

Bearded irises—especially the taller varieties—are so dramatic that they add a "wow" factor to the garden that cannot be ignored. Whether they are planted in small groups or large drifts, it is the color of the flowers that draws the eye toward these beautiful plants. This makes them invaluable to any planting scheme, especially one that is mainly dependent on color.

Generally, bearded irises flower for only three to four weeks. However, this flowering season can be greatly extended if the different types are planted together. The first blooms appear in mid-spring with the Standard Dwarf Bearded varieties, and continue right through to midsummer with the last of the Tall Bearded hybrids.

Standard Dwarf Bearded

The smallest of the bearded irises are the Miniature Dwarf Bearded group. However, these tiny little treasures are not suitable for growing in an open garden border and need to be treated in the same way as alpine plants. In other words, they're best planted in a trough, container, or rockery.

The smallest bearded irises that can be grown in a border are the Standard Dwarf Bearded group. These produce a mass of little flowers that open just above a clump of spiky leaves, forming a low, cushion-like mound of color with blooms that are viewed from above. To increase the amount of color on display, the falls of each bloom splay out horizontally. These irises are ideal for growing near the front of a border. However, as they bloom early in the year, in colder gardens they can be better appreciated if grown in a site that is passed frequently or often visited, such as along the edge of a path or near the house.

When choosing companions for these irises,

look for plants that will grow to a similar size. These could simply be more of the same—in large quantities a mixture of different-colored Standard Dwarf Bearded irises can be very impressive. Spring-flowering perennials such as lungwort (*Pulmonaria*) and grape hyacinth (*Muscari*), or the golden leaves of *Valeriana phu* 'Aurea' will sit happily with the brightly colored flowers of these early-blooming irises. Lamb's ears (*Stachys byzantina*), with furry, silvery leaves, bugle (*Ajuga*), or ground-covering lamiums make excellent weed-excluding companions. However, remember that these are vigorous plants, so leave enough room between each one to allow them to spread. If they start to take over, simply dig them out.

For companions that flower later, look for those that match the spread of the irises—this will be 9–12 inches (23–30cm). The low-growing but mounding herb *Origanum laevigatum* 'Herrenhausen', with its small, round leaves, makes a marvelous contrast to the spiky clumps of the irises. Some of the lower, spreading, and mounding hardy geraniums are also excellent: varieties such as *Geranium* x *cantabrigiense* 'Biokovo' and *G. cinereum* 'Ballerina', both with small, rounded flowers, bloom from late spring into early summer, and will provide a continuation of color. By the time these smaller plants have finished flowering, the taller irises will have begun to take center stage.

Intermediate Bearded

Intermediate Bearded irises flower directly after the Standard Dwarf Bearded hybrids. These handsome plants are taller and much more upright, and produce a large number of well-branched stems with flowers that sit toward the top. Like the Standard Dwarf

Below A mixture of late-flowering, small narcissi and the Standard Dwarf Bearded *Iris* 'Little Blackfoot' and *I.* 'Eye Bright' will grow to roughly the same height, making a welcome contribution to a spring garden.

Bearded irises, they are not usually viewed as individual flowers but as a mass, with the falls of each flower flaring out proudly, as if displaying their color. In size, the blooms are halfway between those of their earlier-flowering sisters and the Tall Bearded irises.

Intermediate Bearded irises tend to be robust plants, ideal for growing in mixed beds with other perennials. They reach no more than 2½ feet (75cm) in height, which makes them suitable for placing in the middle of a border. When choosing companions for them, go for medium-size plants that do not require

staking. The short varieties of oriental poppy are perfect; many more of these have been introduced in recent years. One of the best is *Papaver orientale* 'Kleine Tänzerin', which produces many pale pink flowers that dance on upright stems. The beautiful early-flowering species peonies are also suitable and flower at a similar time. These include *Paeonia mollis*, with carmine-red flowers, and the bright pink double *P. officinalis* 'Anemoniflora Rosea'. Although fleeting, the blooms are carried on short, well-disciplined growth.

In wide borders, Intermediate Bearded irises

may be grown against a background of flowering shrubs or taller perennials. To enhance the color of the irises, it is important to choose the right plant—if in doubt, a simple wall of mid-green foliage will always do the job. Later-flowering perennials such as asters, delphiniums, and tall veronicas will all provide this. These are generally self-contained plants that do not roam far enough to threaten the irises during the growing season.

As Intermediate Bearded irises do not spread to more than 2 feet (60cm) across, they are also suitable for narrower borders. In these situations they can be interplanted with slender, upright plants such as the yellow foxglove *Digitalis grandiflora* or the perennial wallflower *Erysimum* 'Bowles' Mauve'. Biennial wallflowers can also be used to create a colorful swathe that, once ended, can be followed by later-blooming annuals such as love-in-a-mist (*Nigella damascena*), with its wispy flowers, or low-growing, late-emerging perennials like hostas.

Border Bearded

Border Bearded irises, together with Miniature Tall Bearded and Tall Bearded varieties, start to flower as soon as the Intermediates are coming to an end—around the beginning of summer. These can be used in the garden in a similar way to Intermediate Bearded irises, but as they bloom later, they are very useful for providing a continuation of color in the middle of a border from early summer to midsummer.

Similar in shape and size to the Intermediate Bearded varieties, Border Bearded irises grow into short plants that are excellent for viewing at a distance. At one time these shorter plants

would have been discarded because they did not fit into the Tall Bearded category. However, as they proved to be excellent border plants, during the 1950's iris enthusiasts decided to list them under the new name of Border Bearded irises. They produce flowers freely, and these are gracefully borne on sturdy stems. The result is a riot of color that can add life to a mixed border or increase the color and height variation in an iris-only bed.

The flowering period of Border Bearded irises coincides with that of many other medium-size garden plants. *Achillea* 'Coronation Gold', with flat heads of bright yellow flowers, and the small, vivid red blooms of *Potentilla* 'Gibson's Scarlet' make particularly good companions. Taller plants can be placed behind the irises, including lupins and the shorter forms of delphiniums. Any of the smaller plants suggested for growing with

Above When grown together, dark blue Intermediate Bearded irises and rich red biennial wallflowers fill the garden quickly, creating a perfectly balanced picture.

Left Red and purple bearded irises add drama to a path. Once the irises have faded, other plants take command.

the smaller bearded irises can be placed in front of the Border Bearded types. However, as the foliage of these shorter irises tends to be particularly good, foliage-orientated border plants can look stunning with them. These include *Heuchera* 'Palace Purple', which produces mounds of rich red, vine-shaped leaves, and much later, slim stems with tiny, almost colorless flowers.

Miniature Tall Bearded

In style, Miniature Tall Bearded irises are delicate and graceful. Many hybrids that originated in the nineteenth century are now listed as Miniature Tall Bearded irises. In the United States these are referred to as Table Irises since they are particularly good displayed as cut flowers in a vase. However, generally, when any bearded iris is fully open, its petals are extremely brittle, so bearded irises are not often considered for cut flowers.

If you want to use them in this way, the best way to avoid damaging the bloom, is to cut them just before the flower opens.

Since they have much smaller flowers than Tall Bearded irises, Miniature Tall Bearded irises are not nearly as bold or dramatic. The flowers are carried way above the leaves on widely branched stems. These varieties are wonderful for placing in a border among other plants with small blooms. Grown with large flowers, their elegance will be lost. Thus useful companions include *Geum* 'Lady Stratheden', with long, slender, arching stems that end in small, rosette-like flowers, and granny's bonnet (*Aquilegia vulgaris*), which carries its pretty spurred flowers on tall, upright stems. For varieties to place in front of these irises, choose lower-growing, spreading plants with foliage that is slender and flowers that are gentle in color. Candytuft, in its perennial and annual forms (*Iberis sempervirens* and *I. umbellata*), is ideal if planted in quantity.

Above The purple and white flowers of *Iris* 'Wabash' make a truly exciting contrast to the yellow ones of *Phlomis fruticosa*.

Tall Bearded

The Tall Bearded iris is the queen of the bearded iris family. Its tall stems present the flowers high above the foliage, to make a statement that can be seen right across even the largest of gardens. Tall Bearded irises produce big flowers that are extremely glamorous, but most varieties, particularly those of more recent origin, need to be placed carefully. As each plant tends to produce only a few flower stems, it is often better to grow Tall Bearded irises in large numbers rather than singly—a group of anything from three plants upward will make the greatest impact. These should be placed close to each other so that the effect is not too "spotty."

Tall Bearded irises do not like the competition of a large mixed border and,

Above Planting bearded irises in one large area makes a vibrant combination when no particular color or size holds sway. In this scheme the result is balanced yet colorful.

indeed, are often at their most dramatic growing in a bed of their own or with just a few other garden plants. In these situations the background needs to be considered carefully. A backdrop of dark foliage color will set off nicely the handsome flowers of light-colored varieties. Dark-leaf shrubs or the plain green foliage of tall perennials can provide this, and later-flowering plants such as asters,

heleniums, or helianthus also make good foliage accompaniments. The smoke tree (*Cotinus coggygria*), with its mahogany-red leaves, is a handsome companion to irises with red-brown flowers, as are the yellow flowers of Jerusalem sage (*Phlomis fruticosa*) to purple irises. For a more dramatic contrast, orange irises can be placed in front of the bright blue flowers of a tall ceanothus. In front of all these, taller perennials can continue the display of color: the tidy, multi-sprayed blooms of *Astrantia major* or the double, pleated flowers of *Aquilegia vulgaris* 'Flore Pleno' are excellent. These may be planted in large quantities for a simple but striking effect.

Some of the garden plants that do not go with smaller-flowered bearded irises can be used to good effect with the Tall Bearded varieties. Large, dramatic oriental poppies and double-flowered peonies are suitable: if they are similar in color to the irises, plant them some distance away from them; if contrasting, place them close by. Any of the lower-growing companions already mentioned would also be a good choice.

Iris borders

At one time it was fashionable to plant a bed with nothing but bearded irises. Such beds were usually found in gardens with ample space; in today's smaller gardens this may not be desirable, since once the iris blooms have faded the border will contain nothing but green leaves.

However, if space is available there is nothing so breathtaking as a large border crammed full of bearded irises in different colors. The most suitable shape for a formal bed like this is long and narrow. It can be edged with grass and further surrounded by neatly clipped boxwood hedging or backed by a brick wall. The long shape allows different types of iris to be planted so that each can easily be seen. This style of border also allows you to have a succession of bearded irises flowering from early spring to midsummer.

When planting a bed of mixed bearded iris

varieties, place the tallest at the back. The shorter varieties, such as the Border and Intermediate Bearded types, should be positioned in front of these. Right at the front will sit the Standard Dwarf Bearded irises. In broader borders, these dwarf varieties can be interwoven among the taller Median varieties. As Tall Bearded irises produce fewer flower stems than their smaller cousins, the number of varieties used should be limited. In this way you can create more impact. The smaller types, such as the Standard Dwarf Bearded irises, are most effective when planted in groups of three or five.

When planting bearded irises together in this way, some thought should be given to how they are placed. Dark shades can "disappear" if planted in front of other dark irises, so they are better in front of paler varieties. For example, a lilac-colored Tall Bearded iris could be placed toward the back of the border, in front of this you could plant a dark blue Intermediate Bearded iris, and at the very front, a white Standard Dwarf Bearded iris.

Flowers that are too similar in color should not be placed next to each other since they tend to blend into one another and become almost indistinguishable—unless of course, this is the desired effect. A drift of blue bearded irises in varying tones can be stunning; varieties with petals in one color only ("self" types) will stand out better than those with several different colors.

Flowers in subtly blended colors, such as bicolor or plicata types, are better planted near the front of a border where they can be seen. When mixing these with other bearded irises, it is best to plant them with varieties that

Above *Iris* 'Persian Berry' contrasts with dainty French lavender.

Right Restful blues and mauves in the shape of delphiniums, clematis, and irises draw the eye through an arch and on into the garden beyond.

Below No bearded irises produce red flowers, but the brown varieties will often have hints of red which can be brought out of the flower by planting them with other red-flowering garden plants. Here *Iris* 'Caliente' is grown with a ruby-colored *Aquilegia vulgaris* var. *flore-pleno.*

Right Bold colors such as orange and blue are rarely used in the garden as they are sometimes considered garish. But this combination of orange Tall Bearded irises and bright blue ceonothus proves they can be both pleasing and eye-catching.

contain only one color. This should be one of the colors that are present in the bicolor or plicata types.

All bearded irises look handsome when planted along a path. In this situation it is best to limit the number of colors to three at most, and then use only colors that are similar in tone. Kitchen and walled gardens are also wonderful spaces in which to grow all sizes and styles of bearded irises for a dramatic massed effect.

Cottage-garden borders

Cottage-garden borders are designed to provide interest throughout the year. The first flowers begin to bloom in early spring, and some of the earliest of these are the Standard Dwarf Bearded irises. To increase interest,

grow them with other low-growing perennials such as lungworts. These attractive plants produce clusters of flowers that sit above a thick mound of foliage. Since the leaves are often evergreen and heavily spotted with silver, they provide excellent contrast to the sword-shaped foliage of bearded irises. A particularly good variety to choose is *Pulmonaria* 'Opal'. It bears pale blue flowers that sit nicely with iris varieties with softly colored pastel flowers. Other later-flowering small perennials suitable for growing with bearded irises include *Calamintha nepeta* subsp. *nepeta* 'Blue Cloud' and *Sedum* 'Ruby Glow'. Like lungworts, both of these produce foliage and form that contrast with the irises; the *Calamintha* makes a round hummock with very small leaves, while the low, arching stems of the *Sedum* bear red-tinted, gray leaves.

Once the dwarf varieties have bloomed, the Intermediate varieties come into their own. These produce thick clumps that are marvelous with traditional cottage-garden plants such as Jacob's ladder (*Polemonium caeruleum*) and sweet rocket (*Hesperis matronalis*). Both of these varieties form upright, leafy clumps topped with softly colored blooms for weeks on end. A combination containing these flowers will bloom from late spring to early summer, but as the flowers fade, the Border Bearded and Tall Bearded Irises begin their show in earnest.

There is a vast range of cottage-garden plants that can be planted with these early summer-flowering irises. Delphiniums and lupins are traditional choices, but to avoid competition for growing space, these may need to be staked.

If this is a chore, then choose plants that are more controlled in the way they grow. Slender foxgloves (*Digitalis*) are not only well behaved but will also provide height behind even the tallest of varieties. Other more disciplined garden plants might include *Phlomis* *russelliana*, which carries whorls of yellow flowers above mounds of velvety, gray-green leaves, or the Indian physic (*Gillenia trifoliata*), with little white flowers that flutter among a bush of small, pleated leaves. These choice plants are easy to grow and will provide

Left The panicles of a lilac wisteria will grow to form a wall of color that is further enhanced when a narrow bed of the richest purple Tall Bearded irises is planted in front.

contrasting color and form of both foliage and flower to the bearded irises.

The classic plant to accompany the bearded iris is the rose. Modern shrub roses, old-fashioned roses, and English roses are the most suitable since these produce their beautiful flowers on leafy, rounded bushes that will provide an excellent backdrop to the elegance of the Tall Bearded iris. The gentle pink of varieties such as *Rosa* 'Fantin-Latour' or *R.* 'Heritage' are particularly successful with the pale blue varieties. Roses not only provide an excellent background, but grown as standards they can add eye-catching height to a border. The lilac (*Syringa*) is another shrub that complements the bearded iris beautifully. Its flowers are softly colored as well as heavily scented, and with dark blue or white Tall Bearded irises, create a serene effect.

Later-flowering perennials will provide not only continuity of bloom but also green foliage early in the year to enhance the color and shape of the iris flowers. Plants such as *Hemerocallis* 'Pink Damask', *Helenium* 'Moerheim Beauty', and lady's mantle (*Alchemilla mollis*) are ideal. The latest of all the bearded irises to flower are the remontant, or reblooming, types—those that flower at least twice in one season. These can be combined with other early fall perennials such as asters and Japanese anemones.

Finally, once the flowers have faded, the foliage of all types of bearded irises cannot be overlooked. Sword-shaped, it grows into broad clumps that contrast perfectly with larger-leaf border plants such as bergenias, or plants that produce divided foliage like hardy geraniums. Color is also important. Although most iris foliage is mid-green in color, some varieties produce leaves that are closer to gray-green. These are excellent with silver-leaf plants such as artemisias.

Above *Geranium pratense,* feverfew, wild foxgloves, and white irises add height to a cottage-garden border.

Planting and Maintenance

The best time to plant irises is from approximately six weeks after the plant has flowered up until the first frosts, at which point the ground will have become too cold and the rhizome will not produce any further roots. Tall Bearded irises are generally planted from late summer until mid-fall in temperate areas; in places with hot summers and mild winters, early to mid-fall is better.

These are the ideal planting times, as bearded irises produce new roots soon after they have flowered, which is shortly after the old roots have shriveled. There is no reason why bearded irises should not be planted during spring, but since their new roots will not start growing vigorously until early summer they tend not to produce any flowers that year. In general, bearded irises will not produce many flowers until the second year of growth.

Rhizomes

Whether you have received your new plants by mail order, purchased them from a gardening center, or been given them by a friend, all bearded irises are best planted bare rooted. If you buy the plants in containers, plant them as soon as possible, since there is seldom enough drainage for them in pots and bearded irises will die in poorly drained soils. Before planting containerized plants, knock the soil mixture off the roots.

The rhizomes of bearded irises are as individual as the flowers and the size of the rhizome will depend on the growing season, so do not worry if it looks small. As long as the plant has a central fan of leaves—which is usually cut back if it has been sent by mail—then the plant will grow, providing it is given the right conditions.

Growing conditions

All bearded irises prefer a site in full sun, since their ancestors originated in open areas, often with poor soil. However, some of the older hybrids and species irises will grow well in partially shaded conditions. In areas that are extremely hot, the hybrids too will benefit from a little shade.

The soil for bearded irises must be well drained, as waterlogged ground causes the rhizomatous roots to rot. If the soil is wet or contains a good proportion of clay, it is best to plant bearded irises in raised beds.

The type of soil is also important. All varieties will like a well-nourished, neutral soil. They are able to cope with alkaline soils but not acidic ones, which make the roots rot. To correct this, lime can be added. If you are unsure as to the soil type in your garden, it is a good idea to test it (using a soil-testing kit purchased from a gardening center) before planting your bearded irises.

Many of the older hybrids that were to be found in gardens prior to the twentieth century will survive in soils that are deprived of nutrients—for example, in areas that are rocky or partially overhung by trees. However, although they will grow well, most will produce greater quantities of flowers if grown in full sun with little or no competition for nutrients from surrounding plants.

Planting

Most bearded irises should be planted 18–24 inches (45–60cm) apart, although smaller varieties can be placed as close as 9 inches (23cm). Bearded irises grow with the top of their rhizomes above the ground. This allows the rhizomes to be baked by the sun and provides them with the energy required for the production of flowers the following season.

Plant each rhizome with its fine roots spread outward to anchor it into the soil. The top of the rhizome should be just above the soil. If you plant it too deeply, it will either rot or fail to produce any strong growth. However, there is an exception to this rule: in light soils or extremely hot climates it can be difficult to establish bearded irises. In these situations, a light covering of soil, no more than 1 inch (2.5cm) deep, will give some initial protection.

After planting, give the iris a light sprinkling of water. Once the rhizome has become established there is no need to water bearded irises, as they are extremely tolerant of dry conditions.

An alternative method for planting bearded irises so they establish quickly is to plant them on mounds. This is easily achieved by digging two trenches and mounding the soil into the middle. Place the irises on the mound with their roots spread out, then back-fill the trenches, covering all but a third of the roots. Firm the soil around the roots and water in.

Above The rhizomes of bearded irises are swollen stems that creep just below the surface of the soil. They are designed to store enough food for the plant to thrive while it produces new roots. The roots appear once the flowers have faded and serve not only to feed the plant but also to anchor it into the soil.

Opposite New rhizomes emerge at the side of the old flowering rhizome and over the years these will form a broad matted clump. Eventually the old rhizomes will be discarded (see p. 100), leaving the young ones to produce flowers.

Below left Gently lift the established iris from the ground with a fork, shaking off any soil that is clinging to the roots.

Below right Remove the young, healthy rhizomes from the old, central one and discard the old part as it will no longer produce any flowers. Trim the slender roots of the young rhizome back slightly, leaving about 6 inches (15cm) so that the plant can be anchored into the soil.

Bottom left Trim back the leaves into a V-shape. This not only neatens the top but also stops the new plant from falling over in strong winds.

Bottom right Dig a shallow hole and plant the new rhizome.

Fertilization

Bearded irises require only limited quantities of fertilizer. However, if you want to apply nutrients to produce more growth, this can be done in early spring as the plants begin to grow, and again about a month after they have flowered. Bone meal, superphosphate, or 6–10–10 general fertilizer can be used. However, whatever is used must be low in nitrogen since excess nitrogen promotes soft leaf growth and may cause the rhizome to rot. When applying any fertilizer, make sure that it does not touch the roots of the plant directly, as it will cause them to rot.

Dividing

Bearded irises must be divided once every three to four years. If the rhizomes become overcrowded, there will be fewer flowers or even no blooms at all. Varieties that grow quickly, such as the Standard Dwarf Bearded varieties, may need more frequent division.

Division should take place in late summer or fall and can be carried out in two ways. In varieties with large rhizomes, cut the older, central rhizomes away from the main plant, then remove them with a fork. This will allow the newer, outside pieces to spread out into the soil in a natural way. The other, more traditional method is to lift the whole clump using a fork and snap or cut the rhizomes apart. Discard the older, more gnarled pieces in favor of the fresh rhizomes. Cut back the leaves to around 6 inches (15cm) to prevent wind rock and then replant the rhizomes.

Routine care

In the fall, remove any dead or dying leaves to prevent the spread of disease. This is especially important in areas with high rainfall, as the decaying leaves will overwinter the fungal spores that produce diseases such as leaf spot. Old flower stems can also be cut back after blooming; however, no harm will come to the plant if they are left. As the foliage dies back in late fall, the leaves can be cut down to around 6 inches (15cm). Once again, this is not essential, but it does mean that the old leaves will not cover the rhizome and this will help prevent the spread of disease.

Winter protection

In mild and temperate areas, no winter protection will be needed. In areas that are severely affected by frost for weeks on end, it is advisable to protect bearded irises by piling up soil, straw, or leaves around the roots. This will prevent damage caused by upheaval when the soil thaws. However, this winter protection must be removed in spring to expose the rhizome to the rays of the sun.

Pests and Diseases

Root rot

Root rot, also known as bacterial soft rot, is a fungal disease that turns the rhizomes of bearded irises into a mushy, evil-smelling mess. The first signs can be seen when the base leaves begin to turn yellow; eventually they will fall off. There are several causes of this disease, and the main one is wet conditions. Nitrogen-rich fertilizers can also cause this problem, as can insects.

To prevent the disease from spreading, lift the rhizome and cut out the soft, mushy area. Disinfect the wound with sulphur or a solution of 1 part bleach to 9 parts water. Once the wound has dried out, replant the rhizome.

Leaf spot

This is a common fungal disease that appears readily in areas with high humidity and ample rainfall. It is easily recognized by the small yellow and brown spots on the leaf. These gradually spread, and the whole leaf will eventually turn brown. In severe cases, this disease can cause the rhizome to rot.

Leaf spot is often more apparent in the fall when the plant is under stress, but at this time of year it does not have the same disastrous effect. To help prevent the disease from taking hold, clear away any old leaves and weeds that might overwinter the fungal spores. If the problem appears at any other time of year, simply remove the affected foliage.

If leaf spot is prevalent in the garden—and it often is where lots of bearded irises are being grown—prevention is better than cure. Regular spraying with a fungicide from early spring will help: at our nursery, we use two different sprays that are applied alternately to prevent the fungus building up any resistance to the chemicals. Any good gardening center should be able to advise on the appropriate fungicide to use.

Slugs

In temperate areas, the most likely pests to attack bearded irises are slugs. These chew the foliage, leaving holes that allow disease to enter. I use biological control, sinking beer traps into the ground or simply removing the creatures by hand. Slug-killing chemicals are also available.

Aphids

Aphids can be a nuisance and are often responsible for spreading diseases. Chemical methods are the most effective treatment.

Iris borers

In the United States the iris borer is a common pest, especially in the Eastern States. Prevention is better than cure, so an understanding of the pest's life cycle helps tremendously. This is how Schreiner's of Oregon describes it: "Borers begin life as eggs laid on garden debris in the fall. Each spring ... these eggs hatch into larvae. These 1-inch-long (2.5cm) larvae crawl onto the iris and up the leaves. Near the top they chew into the leaves and then down to the rhizomes, where they gorge themselves until they reach a size of about 1½ inches (4cm). Borer injury often appears as notched wounds or slimy wet-looking areas on the leaves. Borers often will hollow out whole rhizomes causing the fans to collapse and the remaining tissue to rot."

Deal with this problem by catching the larvae before their descent. A sharp eye will detect the borer as it enters the leaves, and culling it straight away is all that is needed. Otherwise, spray with a systemic insecticide recommended by your gardening center.

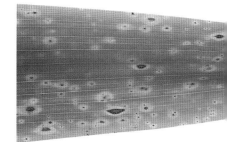

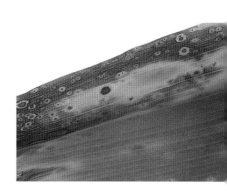

Top Leaf spot is one of the most common diseases in bearded irises and is easily recognized by the brown spots in the leaves. Although not terminal, it does disfigure the plant. Spraying with a fungicide early in spring as well as removing the affected leaves as the spots appear can prevent it from spreading.

Above In this more advanced case of leaf spot, the brown spots have joined together to make larger areas of damage that will eventually cover the whole leaf.

Index

Alizes, 9
American Horticultural Society, 8
American Iris Society, 8
amoena coloration, 6
Annabel Jane, 27
aphids, 101
awards, 8–9
Az Ap, 72

"beard", 5
Beverly Sills, 14
bicolor coloration,
    6, 92–4
bitone coloration, 6
Blackadder, Elizabeth, 7
blend coloration, 6
Blenheim Royal, 50
Blue Hendred, 74
Bold Print, 81
Border Bearded (BB) irises,
    7, 89–90, 92, 94
borders, 92–7
borers, 101
Britain, 7, 8
British Iris Society, 9
Bronzaire, 65
Brown Lasso, 77
buying irises, 9, 99

Caliente, 45, 94
Carnaby, 25
Champagne Elegance, 29
choosing irises, 9
colors, 6, 7, 92–4
cottage gardens, 94–7
Curlew, 62

Dark Spark, 80
diseases, 100, 101
dividing irises, 100
drainage, 99
Dusky Challenger, 37
Dykes, W.R., 9

Edith Wolford, 48
Egypt, 7
Eye Bright, 67, 86

falls, 6
fertilizers, 100
flag iris, 6
fleur-de-lys, 7
Florence, 7
flowers, 6
foliage, 97, 100
France, 7, 8, 9
frost protection, 100

Gingerbread Man, 66
Giverny, 7
Godfrey Owen, 17
Going My Way, 22
Greek mythology, 7

Happy Mood, 72
height, 7
history, 7
Holland, 7
Hot Spice, 69
hybrids, 7–8

India, 7
Intermediate Bearded
    (IB) irises, 7, 86–9, 92, 94
iris borers, 101
Iris flavescens, 63
    I. florentina, 7
    I. germanica, 7
        I.g. 'Amas', 49
    I. pallida, 7, 35
    I. variegata, 60
Italy, 8

Jane Phillips, 26
Jazz Festival, 21
Jeanne Price, 55
Jungle Shadows, 71
Just Jennifer, 78

Kew Gardens, London, 5

Latin Rock, 12
leaf spot, 100, 101
Lemon Brocade, 29
Lilli-White, 79
Little Blackfoot, 83, 86
Luxor, 7

Madeira Belle, 22
Meadow Court, 76
Median Bearded irises, 7,
    57–83, 92
Melon Honey, 69
Miniature Dwarf Bearded
    (MDB) irises, 7, 86
Miniature Tall Bearded
    (MTB) irises, 7, 90
Minoa, 7
Monet, Claude, 7
mounds, planting on, 99

neglecta coloration, 6
nitrogen, 100
nurseries, 9

Ola Kala, 47
Olympic Challenge, 32
Olympic Torch, 55
Oriental Glory, 19
orris root, 7
Out Yonder, 34

Persian Berry, 20, 92
pests, 101
petals, 6, 7
planting, 98, 99
plicata coloration, 6, 92–4
Provençal, 32

Queen In Calico, 30

Raspberry Acres, 71
Red Revival, 18
remontant irises, 97
rhizomes, 7, 98, 99, 100
Ringo, 52
root rot, 101

roots, 98, 99
Rosette Wine, 53
Royal Horticultural Society, 8
Ruby Chimes, 58

Sapphire Gem, 82
Sapphire Hills, 37
Sarah Taylor, 74
self coloration, 6
Serenity Prayer, 58
Shampoo, 64
Sherbet Lemon, 61
shows, 8
Silverado, 51
Skier's Delight, 8, 38
slugs, 101
Snow Mound, 43
societies, 8–9
soil, 5, 99
Song of Norway, 16
Standard Dwarf Bearded
    (SDB) irises, 7, 86, 92,
    94, 100
standards, 6
Starshine, 40
Staten Island, 44
Superstition, 13
Susan Bliss, 41
Sweet Musette, 15

Taj Mahal, 7
Tall Bearded irises, 7, 11–55,
90–2, 94, 97
Titan's Glory, 31
Truly, 9

United States, 8–9

Wabash, 47, 90
War Sails, 25
watering, 99
White City, 42
wild bearded irises, 5
winter protection, 100

Iris Suppliers

Australia
Tempo Two
PO Box 60A
Pearcedale
Victoria 3912

Rainbow Ridge Nursery
Taylor Road
Dural
New South Wales 21

France
Cayeux
Poilly-lez-gien
4550 Gien
Loiret

UK
Claire Austin Hardy Plants Ltd
Bowling Green Lane
Albrighton
Wolverhampton
WV7 3HB

Croftway Nursery
Yapton Road
Barnham
Bognor Regis
West Sussex
PO22 0BQ

Kelways Ltd
Barrymore Farm
Langport
Somerset
TA10 9EZ

USA
Aitken's Salmon Creek Garden
608 NW 119th St
Vancouver
WA 98685

Cape Iris Gardens
822 Rodney Vista Blvd
Cape Girardeau
MO 63701

Cooley's Gardens
PO Box 126
Silverton
Oregon 97381

Maryott's Iris Garden
PO Box 1177
Freedom
CA 95019

Rainbow Iris Farm
250 CR323
Bartlett TX 76511

Schreiner's Iris Gardens
3625 Quinaby Rd. N.E.
Salem
Oregon 97303

Sutton's
16592 Road 208
Porterville
CA 93257

Iris societies

The American Iris Society
Anner M. Whitehead
PO Box 14750
Richmond
VA 23221
United States

The British Iris Society
Clive Russell
47 Station Road
New Barnet
Hertfordshire
EN5 1PR
Great Britain

The Iris Society of Australia
Terry Nisbet
12 Normandale Road
East Bentleigh
Victoria 3165
Australia

Author's Acknowledgments

I would like to thank the following for their help in putting me on the right track: David Schreiner, Cliff Snyder, Rita Gormley, Sydney Linnegar, and Cy Bartlett.

Photographer's Acknowledgments

With special thanks to Barry Emmerson of Leiston, Suffolk, England, whose irises were an inspiration. His *Iris* 'Hazy Jayne' is featured on pp. 10–11. Thanks, also, to Kate Cambell at Eye Abbey, Suffolk, England, John and Lesley Jenkins at Wollerton Old Hall, Shropshire, England, Michael and Sarah More-Molyneux at Loseley Park, Guildford, Surrey, England, and Jan and Rob Waddington of the Kiewa Valley, New South Wales, Australia.